Thoughts Of

A

Church Girl

Thank you so much for your love and support. May God richly bless you.

i

Thoughts Of
A
Church Girl

Latonya P. Grimes

Editorial Midwife Publishing

ORDERING INFORMATION

Quantity sales. On quantity purchases by corporations, associations, and others—orders by trade bookstores and wholesalers, contact Latonya Grimes at Zions.daughter@ymail.com.

EDITORIAL SERVICES

Lita P. Ward, the Editorial Midwife
LPW Editing & Consulting Services, LLC
www.litapward.com

Published in the United States of America

ISBN: 9798704762126

DEDICATION

I dedicate this book to my butterfly. Although you left me when I wasn't ready, you have remained in my heart with reminders of how much you loved me. There are times I wonder why, but I must remember that God's way is perfect. Thank you for protecting me, supporting me, and loving me.

Until we meet again...

ACKNOWLEDGMENTS

To my angels, Mother Katie Bell Little, Keisha Knight and Barbara Matthewson, who watch over me.

To my children, Joshua, Indiya and Asiya who have suffered with me.

To my family that have sacrificed for me.

To my leaders, Chief Apostle Lannice and Apostle Heather Collins, Executive Pastor, Apostle Mary Matthewson, Bishop Travis Matthewson, Apostle Debra Boyd, and my church family, Kingdom Life Worship Center, that have loved all "five of me."

To all of my former leaders for imparting in me.

To Terrell who continually pushes me.

To Sharon who constantly prays for me.

And most of all, to my friends, (I wish I can name them all) who have stuck in there

with me.

Thank you!

TABLE OF CONTENTS

INTRODUCTION

I was having a conversation with a friend of mine one day about life. As we exchanged our different life experiences, she stopped in the middle of her sentence and said, "There is one thing that I thank God that He did not create." I was puzzled and perplexed by her statement. I sat quietly, trying to reason within myself what she meant. I finally killed my curiosity and asked her to explain her theory. She stated, "I am glad that God did not give us the ability to read minds." At that point, I began to understand that behind every smile does not lie a happy story.

Too often, we have the tendency to internalize our feelings due to the positions we hold, our status in the community, or not wanting society to know that we struggle and have issues too. It's amazing how we will go to the doctor, undress for an examination, and answer personal questions with a person we only meet for 15 minutes. However, we will never talk with our loved ones or sometimes to God concerning our inward struggles. It is shocking how people pretend to live in the present, but their thoughts are far away in actuality.

So now, we are about to take a journey with Sini McLin. Sini is in a place where her thoughts have taken precedence in every area of her life. She finds herself struggling with situations, conversing with God, debating with decisions while having these internal conversations with herself. Follow her as she explains her dilemmas and explains her responses as just another "church girl."

CHAPTER ONE

DRESS THE PART

Sunday after Sunday, the same routine: I look in the mirror and examine every part of my outfit. Performing the "up/down test" with my blouses has gotten easier. The "up/down test" was basically looking down to see if anything was looking back up at me. I had to ensure that my breastplate covered those places needed to remain hidden and shielded any area that could potentially become exposed. I decided that wearing ruffled blouses that fit like turtlenecks was my best option. The blouses not only added pop and flare to the whole ensemble, but it elongated my neck and caused me to look taller than I really was. With those added perks, I found myself in a win/win situation. And the questions continued.

Are my nails offensive, or am I adorning myself correctly like a prime and crisp "church girl" should be? Did I choose the right jewelry or purse? Nothing completes a woman's outfit other than the perfect purse that accentuates her style. Should I carry my MK or Coach? Do I leave it in the car or carry it into the sanctuary? Or do I set it beside me or on the floor?

Decisions, Decisions, Decisions...

The flip side of that is that I have never been a fanatic of purses. I have been blessed with many name brands and knockoffs, but I still have not run into my most favorite one. My church bag filled with church documents, calendars, address books, old and new projects, and iPad have been my signature piece for years. I believe the women of my church desire to see me sport a more church right handbag to spice up my femininity. My perception of that comes from conversations and gifts that seem to be everything I do not own or have never mentioned. Each time I am blessed with these gifts, I show my appreciation with a big smile and a thank you because I know that is my cue to step up my game.

Let us not forget the shoes — the most favorite part of my masterpiece. My weekly routine consists of searching for the perfect pair to add flare to what I will be wearing. The higher the heel, the better it feels rings through my spirit each time I put a pair on. It is something about the smell and perfect fit of a new pair of shoes that takes every concern of mine away. Print, color, style, texture — the more unusual, the more I love them. It has become a hobby of mine to search out that "me pair" that causes others to look twice and wonder what she was thinking. It fills my heart with joy to answer those daunting questions: How do you walk in those heels? Where did you find them?" And my favorite question... "How many pairs do you own?"

Finding the perfect shoe is like searching for a rare jewel in the most unpredictable places— consignment stores, yard sales, and stockyards. Obtaining the perfect shoe is like drinking a cold glass of water on a hot day—refreshing.

Nothing tops an outfit better than the right hair to match. Long and brown or short and blonde; curly and red or straight and golden; Bohemian or natural: so many styles and colors to choose from. I may be different from some women concerning hair because my hair doesn't have a lot of value or mean that much to me to the point that I am afraid to cut it, dye it, shave it or grow it. If I lose it, I will buy more. If I do not grow it, I will sew it. Hair is everywhere, so why should I make such a big deal out of mine? The problem that I run into is when my attire is saying one thing, but my hairstyle reflects something else. With my style and preference, some hairstyles, I prefer must compliment a clergy collar. In contrast, other hairstyles will help a plain suit look spectacular.

Taking second and third looks in the mirror had become my ritual. Is my skirt long enough? Are all the curves hidden behind a skirt that is two sizes too big? Performing the "sit test" to measure the precise length of my skirt had become tricky. If my skirt's hem fell at the top of my knees, then my next task was to find a matching lap cloth to cover what could be an eye-catcher or a distraction to onlookers. But if my hem stopped at the bottom of my knees, I finally achieved my goal of obtaining an appropriate hemline suitable for Sunday morning worship service. To be on the safe side, an a-lined, designed skirt was the easiest route because it gave me a perfect hourglass look with the right hem length. It eliminated the potential of a good tongue lashing from my Church Mothers. Walking that gray line has become too exhausting and takes the thrill out of pursuing that ultimate look. I felt the Mothers had this imaginary measuring tape that when I walked in, they could easily detect a skirt that's too short and swarm in quickly like they are the Church's SWAT team. But with grace and wisdom, they would hand me a floral print or lace lap cloth that added length to a skirt that did not meet their expectations.

If I failed their hemline length, without saying one word, they would smile, nod their head, and give me a look that said, "After service, we need to talk." At that point, I dreaded to hear my pastor say amen because I knew I would be cornered and have to explain why my skirt did not meet their "sit test" criteria. I never could give them a good enough explanation of why I missed the mark. I would take the time to explain my ritual to them, how I looked in the mirror, sat down, and stood several times. I even explained how I got my husband and children involved for a second and third opinion. Depending upon how many were surrounding me, I tried different passages of Scripture to ease the blow. If that did not work, I showed them that I brought my shield of faith to persuade them that not only did I know the Word of God, but I did carry it too. I would go as far as telling them that my Bible is like an American Express card; I never leave home without it. I showed them how I had my "sword" tucked in my church bag's side pocket, and I would pull it out like a switchblade. While they tagged teamed me with reprimands, I thought of the different ways of how I carried my Bible. I would have my Bible on the side of my hip as if it was resting in a holster. I also carried it the traditional way, tucked under my arms so the whole world would know I am a Christian!

My church has now become modernized. We have made it easier for anyone to see or read the Word by posting, broadcasting, and displaying the Bible on teleprompters. Also, we provide handouts distributed as we enter the vestibule. Regardless of how it is presented, I still tap my Bible icon, scroll through my list, and find the chapter and verse that has been announced by the Exalter. I find it more comforting to follow along on my iPad as the Word of God is read with power and passion. After this dialogue with myself, I try to refocus on what they were saying and rebuttal my claim. I should not have been surprised that my words did not phase them. Their piercing eyes look through my explanation. Their fingers of wisdom pointed out everything they felt and seen wrong with what I thought was a masterpiece of an outfit.

I just humbly listen to the lecture of what they expected out of me and how to exceed their expectations. As their parade of words bounced around my ears, I started thinking that sometimes or at least once in a while, I wished their expectations included a tailored skirt that stopped right at the knee. One that created a flat stomach and curves that would make any woman wish they shopped where I shopped. Sunday after Sunday, the routine never changes for this church girl.

On my way home, between the fighting of my children and the radio singing to me, I am reminded of Queen Vashti. Queen Vashti hesitated to display her elegance and beauty before a crowd of people. Her opinion and personality caused her to lose out of what was rightfully hers based on her position. I could imagine how she felt when she was met by guards escorting her out of her promised place. I could imagine how she felt each time she looked in the mirror and thought what used to be a blessing to her husband, her beauty, uniqueness, and style had now turned into a misfortune. I could imagine how Vashti now regretted the day that she decided to inform her King that what he found sacred and adorning would not be placed on a showcase to judge before all. Was it really about her uniqueness and style, or was it based on what others thought about her? I wondered how my world would be if I did not allow someone else's opinion to super rule my opinion.

My transition finally took effect when I realized who I was in the Kingdom. Have you ever asked yourself, who am I? Am I defined by my hemline? Am I defined by the length of my hair? Am I defined by the color of my shoes or the brand name pocketbook that I carry? Am I the clothes, or do I make the clothes? When I was able to successfully answer those questions, I realized that there is a certain standard that a church girl should have. That standard is not found in the church manual. That standard is not found in someone's ideology or someone's thoughts and dreams of us. I found my answer in the perfect book that never changes — The Bible, Word of God, or also known as the Book of Truth. I found out that I was fearfully and wonderfully made. Until I accepted my position in God, I would not have obtained my promise in God. When I developed the mindset of who God called me to be, not based on my hemline, hairstyle, or purse, everything else fell in place for this church girl.

SHARE YOUR THOUGHTS

_____

_____

_____

_____

_____

_____

_____

_____

_____

_____

_____

_____

_____

_____

_____

_____

_____

_____

_____

_____

_____

_____

_____

CHAPTER TWO

WALKING THE RUNWAY

Setting my alarm at night does not help me make it to the House of God on time. My Sunday morning routine sound off from my family goes as follows:

"Ma, I cannot find my other shoe."

"Sini, are you cooking breakfast?"

Dog scratching at the door: all of this before 8:00 am. I wonder, does anyone in my house know that I am preparing for service. It's already tough enough to figure out what to wear, but to add all these added distractions is not putting my mindset at ease. Now, I am trying to focus on at least two Scriptures, hum a spiritual hymn, or ask God to take the noise away before all I know to be holy is thrown out the window.

None of this is working because the ticking sound of my clock is getting louder and louder. Then before I can control my tongue, I hear myself scream, "I hate being late!" All of a sudden, the lost shoe is found. My husband is no longer hungry, and my dog runs to his bed. Apparently, my family does not know or even understand the many issues that come with the dilemma of my being late for service.

On my way to church, I debate within myself which door to enter. I know if I enter the main entrance, everybody's attention would be on me. Should I come in the side door, slide in, and sit in a place where people would be wondering, was I placed in timeout or in the corner for bad behavior? Should I enter through the kitchen and walk in with a pitcher of water to place on the pulpit to disguise the fact that I was late? Should I burst through the doors as if I were accepting my award for the latest arriving member? Or lastly, should I tiptoe in and pray that Deacon greased the door hinges so it would not sound like a crying cat announcing my entrance? I begin to laugh at myself for coming up with all these hopeless ideas. Regardless of which entrance I choose, I know there would be some form of attention drawn to me because nothing about me is quiet. My hair is loud. My shoes are loud. My clothes are loud. Everything about me announces to the church that Sini has arrived!

The ride to church can be just as frustrating as dealing with what will happen when I get to church. I am dealing with the fact that I am late, trying not to argue with my husband because he is driving 10 miles under the speed limit. I kindly lean over and say, "Honey, can you please speed up?" His response, "Bae, what's the rush? God will be there when you get there." I respond with a deep breath, rolled eyes, and patting my feet because the response to that would not be good. After what seems to be forever, we arrive at the House of God.

As I walk into the foyer area, I wonder if it is even worth going to church when I know that I am late. As I am walking to the sanctuary door, I hear service has started. Praise and worship have begun. The music is loud, and the praisers are in a harmonic accord. I thank God that I have my husband and children with me because it takes some of the ease off, at least with them. My husband, being the gentlemen, holds the door open to allow me to go in first. Soon as the door opens, everyone turns around as if they are in a choreographically routine led by a choir director giving cues to the singers. I almost feel like the bride walking to the altar to meet her groom or the model displaying the hottest fashion, which demands attention. I wait for photo opportunities as I pass each onlooker while listening to their oohs and aahs. I see people whispering and nudging each other while looking to see what seat I will take. I pretend like I do not notice while others roll their eyes and primp their lips as if I smell funny or did something wrong to them. I continue to look forward while trying to regain focus on my true meaning of arriving at the House of God.

As the usher is walking me to my seat, I reach back to grab my husband's hand for comfort for what I am about to experience. As I reach for his hand, I'm wondering what is taking so long for him to grab my hand. I turn around, and with shock, my husband and children abandon me by finding the first seat in the back of the church. They wave at me to walk with the usher, then my husband smiles while one of my children whispers, "We are sitting with daddy." At this moment, I realize that I am in this alone, and my husband will have a silent ride home.

Although I am a minister of the gospel, I never understood why I had to sit all the way to the front or in the pulpit every Sunday. To make matters worse, the head usher signals to her team where to take me as if she is putting me on display so everyone would see what tardiness looks like, or as if she is walking me to the principal's office to get reprimanded. I sometimes feel like a dead man walking because she grabs my arm so tight as if she has a leash on me and ensures that I cannot run at the first sign of an exit. I try to whisper in her ear that I can sit at the back, but she is determined to seat me where she pleases. What I do not understand is that I was *only* five minutes late. Is this type of treatment really necessary? I would rather pay a fine and sit in the second row from the back rather than endure the humiliation of my tardiness. I take a deep breath and deal with my punishment like a big girl and make a declaration to myself that I will never be late again. I wish I could make that promise, but unfortunately, I cannot.

I remember watching many runway shows, and the model that comes out last is the main attraction, wearing the showstopper. All eyes are on them. Everyone watches in envy of how they want to be them. Onlookers wonder how she managed to be so well kept. Some even try to meet them after the show to find out their secrets. Fans take photos and go home and try to mimic their idol. It seems like the last model had something different about them. It was the way they walked, the expressions on their faces, and the bold confidence that echoed in the room, carrying dynamic power and grace. Their walk demands the room. Now the more I think about it, being late is looking more promising. The stares may turn into opportunities to eventually minister to someone. The photograph maybe my next big break to become an internationally known preacher.

As I take my seat, I look around the room to see who is still staring at me. The Mothers give me that small cute wave. My friend pointed at her wrist as if she had a watch on to remind me that I am late, and the look that I was avoiding was Pastor. He looks at me with that "not again" stare, and deep down, I feel like he will be calling a meeting about my tardiness. I smile back, hoping to change his face's expression, but that stern father-like eye stare remains the same. Now, I begin to get upset with the ushers for not hiding me in the back.

While I am sitting there trying to enjoy praise and worship, I wondered if there should be a section for the ones who are tardy? Now, do not get me wrong; I believe and understand that being in place is key, especially for leaders. I personally feel like the ushers did me wrong by putting me on display. They could have hidden me in the back or slid me in as if I were working in my office. I wish I had a door in my office that led to the outside of the church. Then I would not have to worry about folk looking at me for being late. I could enter in and out through my office, and my secret would be safe. Unfortunately, that is not the case. The ushers treat me like the supervisor on my job — a penalty for being late, loss of privileges for extreme tardiness, and being exposed for not being in my specific place on time.

The tragedy of that is now I have to rewire my mind because when I entered the House of God, the first thought was — Praise. Many enter God's house after struggling with suicidal thoughts, burdens, depression and the list goes on and on. So many enter in hoping to find joy, peace, a hug, or encouraging words. What I must keep in mind is that my presence can be someone's breakthrough. My presence can be someone's deliverance. My presence can be what helps others continue to fight. But it is amazing how my mind can be set and ready to enter the House of God with praise, but the first welcoming sound is the sound of my own criticism. I can enter in with a sound of thanksgiving, but the echo is a sound of chastisement.

Now I am left with a question: what do I do when I make the sound of criticism but expect the sound of praise to echo back to me? An echo is a reflection of the sound that was sent. The sound bounces off matter and can mimic what it heard regardless of where the sound came from. The House of God should be a surround sound of joyous echoes. When the sound of joy is sent out, then that same sound reciprocates back. When the sound of love is sent out, then that same sound reciprocates back. I get disappointed in myself since the sound I want to hear is not reciprocated because I did not send out the right sound.

What I learned that helped me when I find myself being late or tardy going to the House of God is to remind myself that I am not last; I am actually first (Matthew 20:16). Although I do not like being late and the repercussions that follow, I must protect my praise. Suppose I am already entering God's house with a heavy heart or a troubled mind. In that case, the enemy's tactic is to keep me bound and cause me to forget the main purpose: to enter in with a praise, enter in with thanksgiving, and be thankful unto Him and bless His name (Psalm 100:4). Fighting through these thoughts is a task on its own. Avoiding eye contact with Pastor, shaking off the "mistreatment" from the ushers, and forgetting the reminder of what my family did to me is now my new task. I decided to replace my thoughts with the thoughts of God.

I praised like I was the only one there. I sang like I was in the car riding alone. I worshipped until I could feel nothing but the presence of God, and I focused on the preached Word like my life depended on it. After service, I patiently awaited the consequences of my actions.

Pastor just smiled and said, "Do better next time."

My friend laughed at me, as usual, and the usher hugged me and said, "I am so glad to see you today."

To my surprise, the only one that made the biggest issue about me being late was me. I looked at the back of the church where my family was sitting. My husband was talking to one of the deacons while my children were playing with his cellphone. We finally locked eyes. My husband had the expression on his face to cue me that he was ready. I made my exit down the runway. Walking out felt different; I felt more confident and relieved. I gained knowledge that it is time to change my thoughts toward myself.

The ride home was silent. Not because I was still mad at my husband and children for leaving me at the mercy of the ushers, but the silence was because I was pondering over my thoughts and what I learned about myself. You would think that sitting in a high service would cause you to forget or change your mind about things that have happened. The problem I have is that I am analyzing the day's activities, why things happened the way it happened, and what I can do to change it. I can see my husband continually glancing at me while I try to sort out my thoughts. I know he is wondering when his tongue lashing is coming. I laugh within because he looks like he is thinking, *Will you please get this over with before the game comes on at 4:00pm?*

After I finished laughing to myself, I had to change my thoughts to eliminate the possibility of other dangerous thoughts entering in: thoughts of failure, thoughts of not being good enough, or even the thought that God might be mad at me. I had to let it go and just thank God that my family and I made it to the house of the Lord safely.

I had to remind myself that being late is not always a bad place to be. I recall being at the end of the line at school during lunch. It would seem all the good food was gone, and I was left with the worst. By the time it was my turn to get food, the lunch lady had said, "Baby, we have run out of pizza, but this is what I'm going to do. If you can wait for about 15 minutes, I will cook you some fresh pizza and give you an extra slice for waiting." So, waiting long enough can give you double, where people thought you would be counted as the least. Ask Job; it worked for him! Who knows where this walk may lead me? This thought changed my perspective and caused me to smile through it all.

I realized that my husband was still wondering if he was in trouble. I could tell by him continually glancing at me, switching his position from one side to the other, and constantly looking back at our children. So, I decided to let him off the hook. Honestly, it was funny watching him squirm. I wondered if I could cause a tear to fall out of my eye, what his response would be. I started to think, *now that I have him at the mercy of my hands, what can I get for repayment?*

Dishes washed, clothes folded, movie and dinner. The list kept piling, but the Spirit of the Lord intervened. I was trying to bargain with the Spirit of the Lord towards my husband, but I lost that battle. Without looking directly at him, I grabbed his hand and started rubbing his fingers. He did not look at me, but the exchange of him grabbing my hand tighter, letting out a sigh of relief was his cue that he will be watching his football game in peace. I looked in my rear-view mirror to ensure that my children were still sleeping peacefully. How perfectly did this day end as I began to think that I never saw so many advantages by what I thought was wrong. I finally looked directly at my husband and thought, *I am glad that he did not know all the thoughts of this church girl.*

CHAPTER THREE

IT'S WORD TIME

This week has been long and tough. I need a Word from God. I need a Word that will change my perspective towards my job, finances, and how I respond to situations. I honestly can say everything in those areas were tried. After the things I saw and heard, I wanted to walk off my job and ask God, "Why was I there, and what was my purpose"? It really was hard for me to deal with the injustice towards my fellow coworkers and maintain my Christian etiquette while sitting in a meeting that I knew was useless. I sat and pondered, *God, what am I to learn from this?* I need to know why I was seeing and hearing the things that I was seeing and hearing? Although I did not get an answer from God, I prayed inwardly for my coworkers for added strength and the ability to maintain their composure as they listened to nonsense. The expression on my face must have given me away because, after the meeting, one of my colleagues walked up to me and said, "Thank you, I needed that."

I smiled and pretended that I had no clue what she was talking about and continued to walk to my office.

Throughout the day, I glanced through emails, avoided some calls *(Thank God for caller id!)*, and pondered over the changes that were going to happen. I continued to ask God about the purpose and plan that He had for me. When I accepted my position, they gave me a job description, salary rate, and a personalized parking space. I do not have to wonder what I am supposed to do, how it is supposed to happen, or even what the CEO expects from me. My job is cut and dry; no wondering or guessing. One of the questions I have for God is, "Where is my job description?" I understand the ultimate goal is to represent Christ and proclaim the gospel everywhere I go. That's easy. My thought is, what is my personal purpose? Jesus understood His primary purpose — to redeem man back to God; to be crucified for sins that He did not commit. But what is my personal purpose: to travel to foreign countries, preach the gospel, have tent revivals every month, or live a life that somebody wonders why I keep a smile on my face when I get a chance to talk about my Savior?

I have numerous opportunities to talk about Him (my Savior), especially after meetings. My coworkers have nominated me as the sounding board, and my office is the escape room. I took down the sign on my door that read: "Knock Before Entering" because the constant knocking distracts me from completing projects, conference calls, and just plain annoying. Now on my door, I have a sign that says: "Take A Number." So when my coworkers arrive, they look at the available number, then wait until someone leaves before entering. Sometimes, I get a chance to ease a Scripture in and pray for some, but there are a few that immediately tell me, "I do not want to hear about Jesus right now; I just want to vent." So, I listen and pray inwardly.

I must say that since I have started working for this company, my prayer life has increased. I find myself praying about everything and for everybody. When the venters leave, the ironic thing is that they all say the same thing, "I know you were praying while I was talking." I smile and give them an encouraging word and never admit that I was praying. I realize it is the power of God that changes situations, not me. Since I dare not take any of God's glory, I just offer a smile, a hug, let them know I am here for them and pray that they have a wonderful day. But today, I need to encourage myself!

Today, I need to pray for myself. I continue to remind myself to cast my cares on Him, but it is getting hard to let them go. I had to decide to fight through the many voices in my head, the frustration, and the anxiety to stay tuned to God's voice. I know He will answer, but I just wish He will do it quickly.

As I pray for an answer, my door opens, and in walks my first counseling session. I am praying that he cannot read my mind because I wanted to tell him, "Bro, I ain't feeling it today." Before I can tell him how I feel, that small still voice reminds me that feelings are not connected to ministry. I suck it up then listen for the voice of God to direct me on how to help him. After he finishes releasing all the woes in his heart, I give him the Word of the Lord, and he leaves relieved and ready to conquer the day.

Now, I am feeling a little more frustrated because I want to feel how he is feeling. Before I can have an argument with God, my door opens again. In walks another colleague that needs my attention. I suck up my feelings again and become the listening ear that she needs. Of all days, person after person, why has my door literally turned into a revolving door today? I don't have time to argue with God, nor do I have time to complain. I don't have time to have my own personal venting session with God. I only have time to focus on the voice of God to deliver His Word to His people.

Seconds turn to minutes, minutes turn to hours, and finally, it's time to go home. As I walked down the hall, avoiding eye contact with my colleagues because I was still feeling a type of way, and my day was still wearing heavy on me, I heard someone call my name. I played dumb like I didn't hear it and picked up speed as if the building was on fire. My coworker was adamant about getting my attention to the point that she called my supervisor's name, who was walking ahead of me, to obtain my attention. My supervisor turned around and pointed to my coworker to inform me that she needed me. I gave her that "I didn't hear you look" and put on that "how can I help you" smile. My coworker said, "I just wanted to thank you again for listening to me rant today." As she is pouring out her heart in gratitude, my mind shifts to a sermon that my Pastor preached: "If I can just help somebody today, then my day was fulfilled." As she finished her appreciation, I reminded her to thank God and to focus on Him.

On my way home, I picked up the conversation I was having with God while I was at work. I was still waiting for the answers to many of my questions, but none came. With my favorite worship music in the background, a phrase caught my attention and brought me back to the main point—God is able. That one line stuck with me because I failed to realize what "able" meant. "Able" is the ability and capability of performing a task independently. Why am I allowing things, situations, and folk to take my focus off an *able* God? I cannot blame anyone but myself. Sometimes I find myself focusing on what I see instead of what I know—that God is able. The ride home became a time to reflect on an able God. I still had questions, but I decided to put that song on repeat to ease the voices running through my head.

I pull into my driveway and follow my everyday routine: get the mail, throw it on the counter, avoid the screaming voices of my children for 10 minutes, and wind down. However, today was different. When I got the mail, a letter that was on top stopped me in my tracks. I waited until I got in the house to open it just in case I was going to scream or pass out. I opened the envelope and realized it was an unexpected notice from the IRS. If it was tax season, I could understand it, but now I am being audited for what happened three years ago. What in the world?! Now I am debating whether to show the letter to my husband or pretend I didn't see it. I had to quickly encourage myself by reminding myself that God is able. It didn't work at first because I was so bogged down with what my husband was going to say, "How did it happen? How much money we may owe?" Between my thoughts and holding back tears, I had to keep repeating out loud, "God is able." I continued to quote it, even though my spirit had not grasped it yet. So, I decided to leave the letter on the counter so my husband could deal with it.

I was able to make it to my favorite chair in the corner of my bedroom. Sitting there, close to the window, is a piece of Heaven for me. My bay window is aligned with butterflies, soft throw pillows, and Scriptures to remind me of the splendor of God's grace. I stare out of the window as if I am staring straight into the eyes of God. I often wonder if He is staring back at me. It would be amazing to lock eyes with God and feel the peace of Him permeate through my soul. When I have days like this, I need to reach down and remember what the Word of God has taught me. Sometimes, coming up with those words on my own is difficult. Yes, the Word of God is hidden in my heart, but sometimes it's hidden behind what I have made bigger: sadness, despair, worry, and the like. I even ask myself, "What would Jesus do?" Depending on how I feel, the answer is debatable. I try to reason out what part of the Scripture I will use to justify my actions. Should I turn the other cheek (Matthew 5: 38-40) or flip over tables (John 2: 13-17)? Or should I become Peter and cut ears off (John 18:10) or offer all that I have (Acts 3:6)? It's not good when all I have to help me is my own thoughts.

As I sit in my recliner and ponder over this week, I am still grateful for what I really wanted to say and do; I didn't. I am learning to be grateful for the small victories. I remember a time that what was on my mind came out of my mouth. As I reflect over yesteryear, my dog is staring at me as if he knows what I am thinking about. I pick him up and love on him as if to ask him to forgive me for the times I yelled at him. He licked my face as an acceptance of my apology and rested his head on my chest. As this day comes to a close, I am excited about tomorrow—Sunday, because I need a Word.

I really feel like my balance is off. I place things on a balancing scale in hopes of ensuring that everything is leveling equally. The ironic thing about the scale is that it doesn't count the objects; it counts the weight of the objects. One side can have four objects, but the other side can have six. Regardless of the amount, we can put things in perspective by its weight. I often try to prioritize my life by what I feel is important, but what God says is important. My scale should start with the weight of what God finds important in my life. The problem that I have seen and experienced is that I forget that another day is coming. I forgot that on the seventh day, Jesus rested. I am constantly being that mother, active church member, friend, sister, etc. but do not take a day to rest.

Rest is the act of laying aside work to repair, although it seems to be the enemy to me. Rest is the freedom from the force that would cause a disturbance of peace. Still, I constantly miss rest from trouble, rest from distraction, and rest from the inability to hear from God. How can I effectively be in communion with God if I am constantly busy? The enemy's tactic is to keep me occupied. I fail to realize sometimes that there is a difference between quantity and quality. I can do a lot of something but not produce a proficient product.

In the Bible, a lady informed the master that she would be happy with the crumbs that fell from the master's table (Matthew 15:27). Although we will accept the crumbs from God, we should not want to give Him crumbs. The difference between His crumbs and ours is that God's crumbs will last forever. There is power in what He gives us; just one touch can change our lives. Just a glimmer of His Glory changes atmospheres and just a moment with Him feels like a lifetime. My crumbs to Him is like saying, "I took care of everything and everyone else first, and you came second." Why would I want to give my seconds to a God that gave me His first (and only begotten Son)? I must begin to value the rest that God has afforded for me, but right now, rest is the last thing on my mind.

Well, I made it! It's Sunday, and I am anticipating my Word. Nothing and nobody will make me late. Nothing and nobody will distract me. Nothing and nobody will take my focus today. For some reason, I believe my family knew I needed a Word from the Lord. As we left the house to go to church, I saw my dog run to his bed to rest until we returned. My family piled in the car without prompts. My children buckled themselves in without hesitation. I was so focused that I did not pay any attention to how fast my husband was driving. All I was focused on was a Word from the Lord.

As we pulled into the church parking lot, I jumped out of the car, leaving my family behind. Not because I was late, it was because I made today personal. I was ready to hear what God was going to say. I knew that I had a designated seat on the pulpit but sitting there comes with its benefits and disadvantages.

Benefits:

- I will always have a seat. I do not have to worry about it being crowded. Whether I am late or on time, I don't have to worry if I have to look over a big hat or broad shoulders.

- The perfect seat away from the crowd, playing referee with my children and my husband asking, "What did he say?" Away from it all... A place of solace, contentment, and solitude.... A place where I can avoid interruptions...A place where congregants only say a quick hello and find their own island away from the real world and its distractions.

Disadvantage:

- I can see everything. Not only do I see everything, but everyone sees me; every move, facial twitch, and expression. The problem with that is I wear my emotions on my face. My face tells everything. I try to stay engaged and avoid drawing attention to myself. I believe I am getting a little bit better, though. Despite what is going on or said, I normally just smile, nod my head, and avoid eye contact in fear of the truth coming out with a raised eyebrow, a frown, or a small shake of my head. Knowing my actions are visible and can be seen by all, I tell myself, smile, look at Pastor, and smile. It gets difficult sometimes, especially when I am parenting from the pulpit. Today will be different! I am focused and ready.

Praise and worship were awesome. Prayer was wonderful. The spirit really flowed, yet all I am waiting for is the Word. While I am waiting, my thoughts begin to take off. I begin to get frustrated because now I have to fight to focus. During praise and worship, the voices were drowned out because of the music. Now, the Academy Award-winning actress comes forth. Sitting with my feet pressed firmly together, side by side, equal in distance. Shoulder squared, back straight, hands resting in my lap, ready for my cue to read. Yesterday's conversations are dodging between each Scripture and what the Spirit is saying to the church. Pretending to agree by saying, "Amen," but only hearing the argument that I am currently having with myself.

Focusing is getting harder and harder. I glanced at the congregation, trying to get my children's attention to stop them from talking but making sure I hear the keyword to know which Scripture to read next. I now hear the echoes of my husband and I's argument concerning the letter from the IRS. Struggling with the announcement of project deadlines and our new manager's effect on the employees, quickly, I throw my hand up in a wave offering to bring me back to reality, hoping it will help me refocus. Right when I finally can focus on my pastor's voice, I hear him say, "Let the church say, 'Amen.'"

WOW! How did I miss what the Spirit was saying to the church? How did I miss my Word? I was so upset with myself that I allowed unresolved issues to block what I needed — a Word from God. As service was coming to a close, I tried to plot how I would make a B-line out of the church because I did not want to talk to anyone. I was praying no one would ask me about the sermon because I had no idea what Pastor had said, let alone the Scriptures he recited.

Pastor signals the congregation to stand and bid everyone farewell. I speedily gather my things so I can escape to the closest exit. Pastor calls my name and thanks me for assisting him with his sermon. I nodded my head and said, "It was my pleasure." I try to walk away as quickly as possible, but he asks me that daunting question, "What did you get out of the sermon?" I look at him like a deer in headlights trying to remember a Scripture, a phrase, or something to answer his question. Nothing is coming to mind. I pretended like I didn't understand the question and stated," I am sorry, Pastor, what did you ask me?"

With a huge smile, he repeated the question with anticipation of my answer. If I ever needed my children to run to me or my husband to call my name, this is the time. I pulled my Bible out, and with great pleasure, I still had my marker in the place of the Scripture I read. I opened the Bible and stated, "The highlight for me was when you quoted this Scripture. You opened my understanding more and brought clarity to an issue that I was struggling with." Before he could respond, I was inwardly repenting. I had no clue what he said about the Scripture or how it related to me or anything I was dealing with.

He nodded his head to agree with what I said and bid me Godspeed. I felt a good praise down on the inside because of the bullet God allowed me to dodge. I immediately walked towards my husband, so we could leave and go home. Although I was secretly mad with him because of our argument, I still had in my head during service. Out of all the days, he is engaged in a deep conversation about fishing with Deacon. Really? Now, what am I supposed to do? I turn to talk to my children, but they are outside playing with their church friends. I look up to Heaven and ask God, "What did I do to deserve this?" Avoiding conversations with the members is now off the table. I have to be strategic, though, because I do not want to talk about anything concerning the message.

One of the Mothers obtains my attention and signals me to her. As I am walking to her, I pray that the message is not a topic of discussion. Upon arrival, I greet her with a hug and a kiss on the cheek. She looks at me with "that stare." I look back at her like, *why are you looking at me like that*? Mother says to me, "The House of God is a place of release and regroup. You cannot hide your troubles from God or me and pretend that you are alright." I am fighting tears, but I feel my eyes beginning to water up. Mother continued. "Elder McLin, you regurgitated all the things that have happened to you without dealing with the actual issue. It is amazing how you put on your actress-look while sitting in the seat as if you are alright, but it wasn't as shielded as you thought. By now, tears are falling, and I cannot do anything to stop them.

She asked me, "Why do you have to wear a mask in the place where you can be free?" I couldn't answer her because now my tears have changed to a full cry. She allowed me to lay my head on her shoulder and weep. At this point, I did not care who was around or who saw me. I felt like I was lying in the arms of God, and His love captured me.

Mother proceeded. "When Jesus asked the man to stretch forth his hand, the man didn't hesitate but gave Jesus his withered hand. The man didn't hide it nor cover it up; he exposed it (Mark 3: 1-5). Exposure is designed to heal, not condemn. Daughter, in Romans 8:1, the Bible says, 'There is, therefore, now NO CONDEMNATION' to those who believe. It is easy to hide behind a mask or paint on a smile. Regardless of who is around, you must be desperate enough to put forth the withered hand." She then asked me, "How bad do you want it, though"?

I couldn't say anything because the tears were still falling. At the end of the service, I felt like I had missed my Word, but Mother held my Word the whole time. She lifted my head, wiped my face, and said, "Baby, this too will pass." She hugged me, kissed me on my forehead, and hugged me again. I was still choked up and couldn't respond. She nodded her head as if to say she understood. I gave her a partial smile, and she said, "Your husband is waiting. Have a blessed week, and I will see you next Sunday." I nodded my head in agreement and walked away. At this point, I did not care who saw us, how my makeup looked on my face, or even if my eyelashes were still intact. All I cared about was the fact that I received my Word.

When I saw my husband, he looked at me with a smile as if he understood and knew what had just happened. He grabbed my hand, bid his friend goodbye, and we walked to the car. My husband called for the children to come to the car so we can leave and go home. On the way home, my husband asked me if I was alright. I turned and looked at him and said, "Yes, I am great. I got my Word." He smiled and held my hand all the way home. He would squeeze it as if he was making sure that I was still there every now and then.

When we arrived home, he asked me to stay in the car while he got our children situated in the house. It puzzled me at first, and my mind began flipping all over the place. I had all these thoughts and tried to remember any movies that I had watched that resembled the situation that I was in. By the time he came back, I was clutching my purse, hand on the door handle, and sitting at an angle to ensure that if I had to make a sudden exit, I was ready. He opened the door on the driver's side and sat down.

He didn't have the car keys, so I knew we were not going anywhere. I began to scan him for any other objects, looking at his pockets as if I can see through them and focusing on any sudden moves. My husband knows me too well. He looked at me, shook his head, and said, "I told you about watching all those crazy shows. You are looking at me like I am about to do something to you." He then said, "Put your purse on the floor and let go of the door handle." I looked at him while I followed his directions and anticipated the next command. "Give me your hands," he instructed.

Now I remember the movie I have seen that has the same actions. He looked at me and started laughing because he knew I was still apprehensive of his request. He reached over and grabbed my hands, and continued to laugh. I did not crack a smile and explained what he would do next based on the movie I saw. He gave me that look, the one that let me know I better get my thoughts together, or he would leave me in the car all night.

I placed both of my hands in his hands. He gripped them in a way that assured me that he would protect me at any cost. As he held my hands, he looked me in my eyes and said, "Let's pray." I looked at him in a state of shock. Not that he did not pray or have never prayed, but it was how he said it. Tears welled up in my eyes, and I bowed my head and concentrated on his voice. As the tears fell, I felt the presence of God surround us in the car. The peace of God was so overwhelming that his voice started to tremble, and I felt his tears hit my hand. I was overtaken by the love I felt today and to see how much God loved me that He visited me twice. My husband prayed with such sincerity and passion that I fell in love with him all over again.

As he was praying, I was thanking God for whom he had joined me with. After the prayer, he placed my hands on my lap, exited the car, walked on my side, and opened the door. By this time, my vision was blurred with tears, and I had no other trust but to let him guide me out of the car. Before we went inside, he stopped me in the garage and just held me. That made the waterworks flow heavier. He held me until I was able to maintain my composure. As we walked into the house, I was so grateful for the people that God had to speak a word to me and that I was able to change the thoughts of this church girl.

SHARE YOUR THOUGHTS

CHAPTER FOUR

I'M GATHERING MY MIND

I was ready to conquer the world after what I experienced on Sunday. To bask in God's presence is unexplainable. To be able to feel His peace that surpasses all understanding is what I live for. It seemed like the sun was brighter, the birds were chirping a beautiful melody, and everything was giving God praise. Even the atmosphere on my job has shifted. I was eager for someone to come to my office so I could give them an encouraging word, pray with them, or offer them a hug like the one I received. I was ready! I realized more of what Christ meant when he told Peter to strengthen his brother after he was restored. Restoration is that place of freedom that allows one to regain strength and the energy to fight another day. Two days had passed so quickly that I forgot it was Bible study night. My husband called me, and I began making plans with him.

Sarcastically he replied, "I did not know that bible study was canceled." Although I felt crazy and a little embarrassed about forgetting Bible study, I tried to play it off.

My husband laughed and said, "It's alright. I got you covered. Your secret is safe with me."

I immediately responded with, "You are lying. I know this is blackmail information." Sini knew that her husband was going to use it against her at some point.

He chuckled and responded in a smooth tone, "You know that's right, Bae."

I laughed at him, hung up, finished my paperwork, and headed home to prepare for tonight. Once I arrived home, to my surprise, my husband had the children and the dog fed. I started to wonder if I was late or were they just eager to go. Without a lot of conversation, I showered, changed clothes, and informed my crew that I was ready. Everyone was excited on the way to church. They were singing, laughing, and discussing all the great things that happened throughout the day. Maybe it was just me, and I was still on cloud nine, but I truly enjoyed the shift in the atmosphere.

Upon arrival at church, I still had a sense of excitement. I think I was excited because I could just enjoy sitting with my church family in a relaxed environment. Bible study is fun with no real expectations. You do not have to worry about the protocols of church; just fellowshipping and learning. Plus, this is the only time that I get to blend in with the crowd. There are no Sunday morning type interactions: talking to the neighbor, high-five three people, fan someone, etc. Just calm basic teaching and listening.

We walked into the conference hall. As usual, it was crowded, filled with spectators anticipating what God was going to say. While scanning the room, I see some talking; others are reading, children playing, and the rest sitting quietly awaiting the entrance of Pastor.

I'm so glad I didn't have to worry about those things because I was really excited to be there. Tonight is the night that I take self-inventory and ask God those daunting questions that will help me grow and figure out the next steps that I need to take to please Him. I know this will occupy my mind for one hour and a half, even if Pastor adds on an extra fifteen minutes. Although the crowd consists of about 65 people, I wonder what is going on in their minds.

Before I get into a deep conversation with my thoughts, Pastor walks in and greets his students. Everyone responds, claps their hands, and the excitement in the room spreads. I prepare by placing my tablet on one side and iPad on the other. My pen and highlighters surround me to ensure that I do not miss an important nugget. On the other hand, my husband shakes his head, giggles, and places his Bible in front of him with his hands resting on the table. I wondered why he giggled at me. He normally asks me for something because all he thinks he ever needs is his Bible. One day, I'm going to decline my supplies to teach him a lesson, and hopefully, he will stop laughing at me.

Bible study has begun, and instantly my thoughts pick up from where they had stopped. I look at Deacon and wonder does he really have joy like he testifies every Sunday. Does his heart really get excited every time he enters the House of God? Although his son is in jail, his teenage daughter just got pregnant, and his aunt will be funeralized on Saturday, he seems happy. He got a smile on his face but is it really real? I take a glance at Mother. She is sitting all poised with her floral dress and sandals that are firmly laced around her ankle. Every time somebody mentions Heaven, she displays a look of inner peace. Then you can see water form at the bottom of her eyelids. I notice how the other ministers are attentively taking notes as Pastor discusses the revelation of the Word of God. They have this look of hunger as if they are pulling the words out of Pastor's mouth. They feed off what Pastor is saying, like a newborn nursing on his mother's breast. Just to watch the eagerness in them made my heart glad. When I was first ordained, I remember that was me—hungry, in anticipation, eager, and with zeal. Watching them caused me to focus on where I am and where I would like to be.

I remember when I first started my ministry assignments, everything was scheduled around Bible study. I understood that Bible study was when I was able to ask questions, get an in-depth knowledge of God's Words, and co-mingle with people who wanted it just as bad as I did. I was able to ask those hard questions that people were afraid to ask:

1. Did dinosaurs really exist?

2. What was the color of Jesus' sandals?

3. What did they season their meat with when they had those large barbeque feasts?

Those questions were the ones that only a skilled, educated theologian had the answer to, and I was determined to find out the answers to my questions. I wanted to know everything. I did not care if it sounded crazy to anyone. But then life caught up with me. Life's issues sent me in a tailspin, and life caused me to look at reality from a different perspective. Reality taught me that some things only come through fasting and praying. Don't get me wrong! I still desire Bible study and strive to be there every night. Still, I struggled with emotions, wondering if life is worth living. Ready to just walk away at one point had become my new norm.

At that time, I realized that it was easy to look attentive. However, when your thoughts wonder how you will make it from day-to-day, eventually, the color of Jesus' sandals did not matter, nor the genealogy of dinosaurs. I am so glad that God did not give us the ability to read minds. I found myself focusing on my transition from there to here, that I really have no clue what Pastor is teaching. Every now and then, I glance at my husband's Bible to make sure I am on the right book, chapter, and verse. I realized I need to write something so it will look like I am engaged. Once I caught up with the Bible study lesson, I went back to my private session with God.

I realized that coming to church, learning about God's Word, and quoting Scripture was not enough for me. I needed to learn how to deal with life. Life had a way to remind me that I was human. Life was an expert at teaching me that we should not only be God-conscious but life conscious too. My friends would tell me all the time, "You live on earth, but you work to get to Heaven. Don't forget to live here." Yes, my goal is to make it to Heaven. Yes, my goal is to strive to be all God will have for me to be, but I had to learn to balance both lifestyles. I am a spiritual being living inside a natural body. I found myself becoming extremely spiritual that I felt all I needed was Jesus and Jesus alone. I had to be honest with myself and figure out the void in my life that caused me to think a certain way.

I'm learning that it is okay not to be okay, but I have to do something healthy, so I will be okay to receive those things that God has for me. As my conversation with God was getting more intense, I realized that my husband had moved to another

Scripture. I immediately followed his actions and hoped I landed on the same chapter. As I was scanning my iPad, hoping that I would land at the right place, I heard Pastor call my name. My heart started racing, and my hands started trembling because I knew I was not prepared for what he would ask or say to me. I looked at him with puppy dog eyes, hoping that would ease the blow. He asked me to come to the front and elaborate on a passage of Scripture. I almost fell through the floor. I walked slowly to the front, praying that he would give me a clue on the Scripture that he wanted me to elaborate on.

When I arrived at the podium, he said, "Elder McLin, please elaborate or explain in your own words the revelation you received from the Lesson Scripture." I stood there like a deer in headlights. I looked at my husband, hoping he could give me a clue, but he was staring back at me with a smile on his face anticipating my response. I was trying to figure out how to ask a question to get a clue of what the Scripture was, but I could not come up with a logical response. I finally decided to just fess up and admit that I had no clue what the Scripture was. As I was about to acknowledge my fault, the timer signaled that Bible study was over.

Whew, saved by the bell! I was the happiest woman in the room.

At that instant, I appreciated my Pastor more than ever because he is very structured. I looked at him as if I was so hurt that I could not respond to the question. He apologized for not giving me enough time to answer the question, but he would give me another chance. I nodded my head and walked quickly to my seat to gather my things and leave. On the way home, my husband began to chuckle. I asked him what was funny. He stated, "I knew you had no idea what the Scripture was." He continued and stated, "I could tell how you were looking at me." He began to laugh hysterically without any regard for my feelings. I looked at him, rolled my eyes, and tried to hold back the laugh that I had on the inside. I didn't think he could tell, but unfortunately, he knows me. The more I thought about it, I realized that he had two blackmail cases on me in one day. How did I let my guard down? Now I will be in his debt for a while. I kept looking at him, hoping he would stop laughing but to no avail, he wouldn't. I eventually started laughing at myself and realized what happens when I allow my thoughts to get carried away by this church girl.

SHARE YOUR THOUGHTS

CHAPTER FIVE

FATHER'S DAY

Well, another holiday is fast approaching, and I find it difficult to relate to it. When it comes to my husband, I can scream, shout, do a dance, and enjoy the day. But, when it comes to a personal flashback, I see Father's Day like another day. My ritual to celebrate my husband is breakfast in bed, gifts, a fun-filled day, more gifts, and quiet family time in the evening. I have no problem honoring those that I feel deserve it. The problem comes in when I have to remember what I did not have. I watch as many people honor, respect, and celebrate the person that gave them life. The person who protected them from fears and the person that assured them that they would cover them in the midst of any storm they encountered. Yes— their father. A person who I have never met. A person who I have no clue how to introduce or even appreciate. A person who I do not know how to define or recognize if he stood in my face and smiled. I wonder what it would have been like to have one of my very own.

Someone who could relate to me and really understood me. Someone who I could count on to protect me and genuinely love me because he sees himself in me. Well, unfortunately, I will never have the pleasure of knowing.

I never blamed or was upset with my mother because of my father's absence. I realized that no one could force anybody into a relationship that they do not want. When I was younger, and this particular day drew near, my mother would assure me that I was loved. She would do something extra special for me on that day, so I would not feel slighted by my father's absence. As I got older, I tried to find the good out of the holiday. I began to tell myself that at least I saved money and was able to buy myself that gift I waited patiently for. I do not have to worry if he did not like his gift, if it was the right color, the right size, or the right brand name. At least that is one disappointment I can scratch off my list because this Father's Day will be perfect like the others—no worries.

My No Worry List:

1. No worries if he would really love his gift
2. No worries if he would actually wear it

3. No worries if he would enjoy the well-prepared dinner
4. No worries if he would exclaim to the world that he has the best daughter ever
5. No worries if I would still be Daddy's Little Girl

What became difficult for me when I gave my life to Christ was to see God as my Father. See, that concept left me in a state of confusion because the One now that I am supposed to trust is being compared to someone I cannot relate to. I would get aggravated when I would hear someone say God is my Father. I would immediately think about all the crying days, disappointing times, heartbreaks, etc. And now an evangelist is trying to convince me that I should trust God who is my Father? Well, I don't think so.

Now, I have always been a church girl, but there were some areas that I needed to mature in. One Sunday, we had a guest speaker. She was preaching about God's love and how He will take care of us. She had my attention, and I started feeling this warm sensation all over me.

Exalter: "Your Heavenly Father loves you!"

Me: "Amen!"

Exalter: "Your Heavenly Father will provide for you!"

Me: "Amen!"

Exalter: "Your Heavenly Father cares for you!"

Me: "Amen!"

Exalter: "Your Heavenly Father will never leave you!"

Me: "Amen!"

Exalter: "Your Heavenly Father will be just like your earthly father!"

Me: Blank stare... Rolled eyes, lost focus, and ready to leave.

At that point, I was wondering if she knew what she just did. Did she realize that she lost me? How can I relate to my Heavenly Father when compared to an earthly father? How can I trust a Heavenly Father when I do not trust an earthly father? Hellooooo Preacher Lady! Over here! Please look this way! I cannot trust, relate, or count on someone I have never had a relationship with. Now, I am stuck. I wanted to visually show her what she did. In my thoughts, I put up this visual diagram...

Earthly Father	Heavenly Father
Left me...	Would You leave?
No relationship...	How can I have one with You?
No trust...	How can I trust what I cannot see?
No honor...	How can I honor whom I cannot see?
No provision...	How do I know You will provide for me?
No stability...	How can I believe You are there?

In my confusion and hurt that Sunday, I wanted to scream out to her that this church girl did not have that experience. If I could just have been able to tell her this, maybe she would have gained insight and more clarity... *"It's amazing how our Heavenly Father is portrayed as the Redeemer of the world, but compared to an individual with no stability. And now you want me to trust someone [God] compared to someone else I do not know? Wow! But, it's not you; it's me."*

She just did not understand that growing up without a father has been a recurring conversation with my friends and family. I didn't want to tell my mother how I really felt because I did not want her to blame herself. I just accepted her tokens of love and protection and pretended like I was okay.

If I had a chance to have a heart to heart with my father, I would tell him... *"I really believe you do not know the damage you have caused due to your absence. You were designed to protect, care for, secure, and demonstrate what I should look for in a man. Your job was to scare away the Boogie Man, fight off the boys that I thought I fell in love with, and teach me how to say no to the cute guy that lives next door. Your role in my life is so important that it is a direct reflection of what God is to His children. Matthew 7:11 and Luke 11:13 discusses how a father should give good gifts to their children. In those passages, good gifts are connected to what the Father does. A gift is freely given without price, expectations, or rewards. A gift is given from a place of gratitude with the other person in mind; it's not just during holidays or special occasions. Gifts are designed with the recipient in mind. Christ gave us a gift that is beyond repayment. He sacrificed all that He knew and had to give us eternal life, not only eternal life in Heaven but a prosperous life on earth. There were no boundaries to His love. There were no expectations for the cross. All Christ was concerned with was our well-being. When I take those variables and compare them to the relationship that we are supposed to have, why shouldn't I expect anything less from you?"*

I had many father figures in my life, and I love each of them dearly, but for me having father figures is entirely different from having a father. Because of my territorial mindset, I could not fathom the fact of sharing someone's dad. It was hard to understand why this man could not belong to me. He treated me like a daughter. He called me his daughter. He acknowledges me as his daughter, but unfortunately, he was not mine. I had to watch him care for his children, walk away from me, and then acknowledge his actual role in my life—uncle, cousin, pastor, etc.

I did not have free access to them. I could not go out on those father and daughter dates. I could not call him in the middle of the night and tell him about the bad dream I just had. I could not go to his house, put my feet on his couch and cuddle under him until I felt better. I was robbed of those conversations that would guide me to make the right decisions in dating. I was not able to cry on his shoulder after I had been mishandled by some ignorant man who did not value my worth. Being angry about not having my own dad is an understatement. It left me void and empty inside. It left me questioning my own existence, and to have to share a dad was the least of my desires.

Finding solace in a loving God has helped me to cope with the absence of an earthly father. I often wonder what my life would have been like to have a dad of my very own. I decided to stop wondering and accept that my Heavenly Father loves me unconditionally—flaws and all. I am saddened by the fact that a man wanted a daughter like me but never met me. I am saddened for the man that lost the opportunity to receive love from a little girl who only wanted a father in her life. I am now saddened that my father missed the opportunity of being the best dad he could be to the best church girl that I have become.

SHARE YOUR THOUGHTS

CHAPTER SIX

IT'S A CELEBRATION

Well, Father's Day has come and gone; now it's time for a real celebration...my birthday. Yes, the national holiday that is celebrated everywhere! Well, not exactly, but that is what I think. Not wanting to have a party or a family dinner, I decided to do something different for my birthday. I wanted to reflect, write a letter to myself, and be honest about my journey. I often reflect on my life, but it seemed this was a great place to start a new chapter. I realized that true feelings come when a person is honest with themselves.

While lying in bed, reflecting on how and what I was going to write, I heard a knock at my door. I reached my hand over to tap my husband to ask him to open the door, but he wasn't there. Engulfed in my thoughts, I had not realized him not being in bed. After hearing another knock at the door, I yelled out, "Come in."

When the door opens, I am met with screams of birthday songs, balloons, flowers, gift bags, breakfast, beautiful smiles, and my dog. I laughed, cried, and hid under the covers. I did not expect this much attention this early in the morning. My husband dug me from under the covers while my children jumped on the bed. As I came from under the covers, my dog was waiting to lick my face. Somehow, I believe she knew what we were celebrating. Pleasantly surprised and grateful, I was speechless. Normally, the celebration would start once I am showered, dressed, with a full makeover since I had to be camera-ready. However, today it wasn't about pictures. It was about love and gratitude.

So, after the birthday shenanigans, I explained to my family that I needed to sit in the office and take time for myself. They understood and gave me my private time. I heard my dog following me, so I turned and had a heart to heart conversation with her. She even seemed to understand. When I entered my office, I honestly felt a spirit of peace. I took the time to read all the inspirational plaques and pictures that helped me start my reflection moment. Instead of sitting at my desk, I sat and propped my feet up in the lounge chair accented with purple butterfly pillows. With paper and pen in hand, my thoughts started flowing. As my thoughts flowed, I began to write:

What have I learned about myself? Well, this birthday started as I expected: new resolutions, new dreams, new plans, new directions, etc... the typical new birthday start. The twist came in when different experiences changed how I viewed the world and how I viewed others. I didn't see a big difference in the beginning because my "normal" did not change work, church, school, and home, but when I had to take a break from it all, I started to see and feel the switch. Relationships were questionable, faith walk was tested, and who I am called to be was challenged. As days turned to weeks and weeks turned to months, my thought and focus turned to me. That daunting question: Who am I? started to be a recurring question. At one point in my life, I didn't know how to answer it. I was able to describe what I did but not who I am. I identified myself as the things that I did or the character I played in others' lives. Still, I did not know how to identify myself as me. I know my favorite color because I adopted it from a traumatic experience (which, from time to time, still makes me cry).

I know my favorite food because it's the only consistent thing I have eaten since I stopped eating meat. I can even identify my favorite insect because it reminds me of a piece of my heart that broke. However, I had the daunting task of identifying myself. So, now I have to answer the question; Who am I? Once I am truly able to answer that question, I can honestly answer what I have learned. Well, I am a woman who never was honest about how she truly felt because of fear of rejection. The rejection came from the experience I had in my childhood. My father never accepted me, acknowledged who I was, or spent time with me.

On top of that, I had to watch my siblings interact with their fathers. To add insult to injury, when my mother got married, they had two children, so I lived with it for a short period of time. I pretended that it did not bother me, and I looked in other directions for comfort. I developed issues such as emotional eating, low self-esteem, loneliness, and rejection. I believe I went through a period of depression because being alone was alright with me. I later realized that I brought with me the feeling of wanting to be loved into unhealthy relationships. Anyone that showed me love, I became attached because I wanted it so bad. I am a woman who struggles with consistency and discipline.

When things get hard or do not go as planned within my timeline, I want to give up. Not only that, I became a woman who would compromise who I am just to make others happy. This trend was seen at home, in relationships, at work, and in church. Unfortunately, people did not get the authentic me. The sad part about that is I started to wonder who the authentic me was? I felt people could not handle my flaws, my crazy, *or even that soft side that had been abused, misused, and abandoned. It got so bad that I didn't know what real love was.*

So, what I learned about myself was that it is perfectly fine to be me. I learned it is perfectly fine to not be okay. It is perfectly fine to make a mistake and ask for help. It is perfectly fine to want love and receive it. It is perfectly fine to love myself and expect to be loved. It is perfectly fine not to compromise and set expectations on how I should be treated. It is perfectly fine not to be everybody's cup of tea because everybody does not drink tea. It is perfectly fine to take risks and chances. It is perfectly fine to accept who God has made me to be, and it is perfectly fine to be free!

As tears flowed down my face, I realized how much I have robbed myself of being me! Through many mistakes and accomplishments, I realized that God had been by my side the whole time. I put the pen and paper down and just wept as I completed the thoughts of this church girl.

SHARE YOUR THOUGHTS

CHAPTER SEVEN

DANCE LIKE DAVID

Having a conversation about service with my husband is sometimes a comedy act. He sees the things that I do not see and hear the things I do not hear. He constantly tells me I do not pay attention because I am wrapped up in what is going on during the service. I often agree with him because I just love the dynamics of worship. For me, the favorite part of service is the praise and worship service. Ten elephants and a giraffe can walk through the middle aisle, and I would not see it. I am engulfed in the presence of God and the flow of the Spirit. This Sunday was no different.

Praise and worship service was off the chain. I wish I had the voice of angels or could sing like those world-renowned artists. I know why I haven't been asked to join the team because my voice is not equivalent to a singer. I could see the many faces if I grab a microphone and begin singing. I can hear them saying," Baby stay in your lane. Go take several naps; forget the seats. You didn't wake up on the wrong side of the bed; you just didn't wake up." So, with humble submission, I gracefully stay seated in my decorative seat aligned with brown course wood, cushioned with soft, green linen, and wait.

Song after song, praise after praise, worship after worship, I thought to myself, *I wish I could sing or direct like I see many people do in a concert.* The choir sounds so good that I want to ask people, "Do you know that victory is in your praise? Don't you know that you were created to worship? Don't you know that everybody can do it? The only thing that is required is a breath. I wondered if praise and worship service was a class, how would it go? As the thought travels through my mind, I hear the music start.

I got tickled because it seemed like they heard me, and the classes started. The first class was taught by the praise and worship team. The instructions start with a series of questions— "Are you happy to be here this morning? Did God wake you up? Did He do anything that you are grateful for?"

If there is no response, then it moves to directions— "Come on! Put those hands together and bless God with the fruit of your lips by telling Him, 'Thank you!'" And if that doesn't move the saints, they tell you to grab or talk to your neighbor. I think they are doing that to wake up the folks before the visitors come.

The next class (for the advanced group) was held by Pastor. He starts off with a testimony about how someone was sick, followed by Scripture to back up the testimony. Then, he erupts to— "What if that was you?!" The advanced praisers immediately start bucking (church term for shouting/dancing) while he continues to prompt the intermediate and beginners. Once the whole class catches the revelation, help comes—the ushers. They guide, fan, and wrap. They look around to ensure no accidents, head-on collisions, wardrobe malfunctions, or any sorts of foolery during this explosion of thanksgiving. The musicians don't add any relief because when everything is calm, the advanced praiser hears that key change and erupts in another round. By this time, the intermediate and beginners are done and just wait for the next portion of the service. I'm wondering if they are "taking notes" to be promoted to the next level.

Sometimes I just stand and watch to see the move of God on people's lives, but today, I'm clapping, I'm jumping, and I'm screaming. I am in a building filled with a group of folks that is full of gratitude and thanks. I feel like the seasoned saints when they say, "When I think about the goodness of Jesus.... If I had a thousand tongues......"

When there was a battle, the praisers were sent first (II Chronicles 20:21) along with the musicians. It is kind of weird to send people to fight when their only weapon is praise. When I first heard that Scripture, I did not understand what it meant. I honestly thought they were sent as a distraction until the real army came in and fought. I almost asked God was He setting them up for a downfall. I thought the praiser's job is to set the atmosphere for what is about to happen and to thank God in advance for what He was going to do.

But after I matured in the gospel, I realized that my purpose is to thank God for something that has not happened yet. I am glorifying God for the future. I am giving Him praise for what is yet to come. Advanced praise is letting God know that there is total trust and sufficiency in Him. Regardless of the situation, regardless of the circumstance, regardless of the report, my praise will outweigh it!

Worship is a totally different ball game. Those that worship Him must worship Him in spirit and in truth (John 4:24). My flesh praises God, but my spirit worships God. I understand that there is a place in God that my flesh cannot go. This place is behind the veil. To go behind the veil, I must prepare myself mentally and spiritually to enter in. Praise is easy. Let the right thought, the right music, and the right sound ring out, and praise will erupt. But when there is true worship, it does not require music or a sound. It is an intimate place between the worshipper and God. It is a place of calm and solace, where nothing else matters. Worship is that place where a worshipper loves on God and God loves on them back, a place of true submission to the Spirit. The mercies of God are found in true worship. The divinity of God is found in true worship. The believer's goal is to be trapped in a place that is indescribable or imaginable. Worship is a place that the worshipper gives God love for just being God. What more joyous view is to be in one place, on one accord, worshipping jointly together? How good and pleasant it is for brethren to dwell together in unity (Psalm 133:1)!

For me, worship is my place of escape. Being in the presence of the Lord allows me to rest in His love, and I am able to cast all my cares on Him. I often imagine the place of worship like Heaven. The place where it is just God and me. Now I understand what my husband means. I do not see anything. I do not hear anything. I am in that place with God, trapped in splendor and grace. I wonder if anyone understands how it feels coming from the thoughts of this church girl?

CHAPTER EIGHT

LET THE CHURCH SAY, "AMEN!"

I received a phone call from Pastor that typically makes me nervous—preaching assignment in two weeks. Why do I get so nervous? Why does my stomach begin to ache and my head begins to hurt? Why do I feel like I want to call in sick or ask him if he dialed the right number? I know I am well prepared because I study even though I don't have an assignment, and I pray daily. I fast at least twice a month. What am I missing? It finally dawns on me why I feel like a runaway bride—I think about all the times I missed the mark, and how jacked up I really am. Nevertheless, I shouldn't let that hinder me or cause me to second guess who God called me to be.

I wish goodness or a reasonable amount of money would work that would cause Pastor to change his mind, but unfortunately, he will not take the bribe. I remember the last time I got the call, and I asked my husband if we could do something special for Pastor and his wife. With his approval, I came up with a brilliant plan to get out of the assignment. After service, we took them out to their favorite restaurant, paid for their meals, and presented Pastor and his wife with new bible cases with their names engraved in gold. I should have felt guilty, but honestly, I didn't. I was so overwhelmed with fear that I was trying to abandon the call by any means necessary. Of course, I did not tell my husband about it, or he would not have gone along with it. So, I kept this master plan to myself and prayed that it would work out in my favor. My intentions were pure, but to be honest, my motives were supposed to assist me out of what brought fear to me.

The joy on their faces was priceless. As we left the restaurant, I was trying to figure out a way to suggest to him to allow one of the other ministers to preach. He let me finish my proposal and stated, "Elder McLin, my wife and I are so honored that God placed your family in the ministry." He continued to thank us for our hospitality and gifts. He closed his gratitude with this statement, "I am anticipating the Word God will speak through you next Sunday."

With a blank look on my face, I nodded my head and walked to the car. I looked up at Heaven, and honestly, I thought I heard God laughing at me. I decided to forfeit my thought of exiting, bite the bullet, commune with God, and wait for a Word. I waited and waited and still waited. I start to wonder if God knows that I am waiting. I don't want to preach anything out of my flesh, so I'm calling on God, but He isn't answering, so I'm getting desperate now. I started hoping the service was canceled or developed some type of ailment that prohibited me from ministering. That did not work, so I started to develop an escape plan that if Plan A and B don't work, I can blame it on my car for not showing up for service.

Three days before my assignment, out of the blue like a falling star, I hear a small voice say: "Keep it real." I'm puzzled, bewildered, and more nervous than before. My questions are: Which way do you want me to go, what Scripture, what character, and how am I going to execute this? I'm so confused that now I wish I had not heard the voice. As I continually question the onset of this topic, I hear that small still voice say again: "Keep it real." I suck it up, search, research, edit, compose and delete. All the while, I pray what I think is a complete sermon does not turn out to be a big disaster.

As I arrive at church, I receive the accolades of a famous televangelist. My armor bearer meets me at the church double doors and takes my robe and briefcase. I am escorted to my office (as if I don't know where it is) to mediate and change into my clergy attire. What she doesn't know is that I am still apprehensive about the message. My armor bearer is sitting in silence, waiting for her next instruction. I honestly want to ask her where she was last Sunday when I had to bring in those boxes of Sunday school books by myself. Where were you when I couldn't zip my skirt, and my children were nowhere around? Where were you when my husband had to work? I was left completing the church bulletins alone. Why now? I knew it was my nerves talking, so I just repented and began to be grateful that she was there.

It's time! I've prayed, reviewed my notes, and gotten dressed. I hear praise and worship beginning, so I know at any minute Pastor is going to knock on my door and escort me to the pulpit. As I gather my thoughts, I hear a small tap on my office door. My armor bearer opens the door and welcomes Pastor into the room. At that moment, I look for an exit, a trapped door, or a window that I can jump out of. To my despair, there isn't one. I am stuck with delivering a Word that I am nervous about.

As we walked out of the office into the sanctuary to the pulpit, and the fight began! The adversary began to remind me of all the negative things concerning me. I began to throw every Scripture I can think of to kill the thoughts that he was trying to get me to adopt. With God on my side, I won the victory just in time for Pastor to call me up to the podium to preach. I walk slowly, heart racing, hands sweaty, knees buckling, and ready to exit left. With 400 eyes looking, 400 hands clapping, and 200 lips moving, I decided to stay.

I gave my honors, read my Scripture, prayed, started with a testimony, and one talk to your neighbor. By this time, I feel like me—focused on souls and ready to deliver this Word from God. My sermon normally starts off with a narrative of the who's, why's, and when's, but this time it was different. I began with a character and expressed their inability to "do right" and how their faults affected their family. But the heart of the matter is we are all human and have faults. I proceeded to inform the crowd about the good side of doing what is right. Then all of a sudden, I feel a shift in my spirit. I'm standing there in a pink outlined robe, adorned with diamonds, flared out sleeves with a high raised collar. Just as I am about to hit a climax in a part of my sermon, I hear the Spirit say, "Take the robe off."

I began to hold a conversation with Holy Spirit while adlibbing the remainder of my sermon. The congregation is going wild, people are screaming, and some are shouting. The music is playing, and I continue to hear, "Take the robe off."

I tell Holy Spirit, "That is not protocol. I can't do that. I will get reprimanded. Can I please finish this sermon and sit down?"

Holy Spirit repeated the command, and I graciously began to unzip my robe. I refuse to look at Pastor or my armor bearer because I cannot deal with their reactions. Nor did I want to read their lips as they asked what I was doing. As I follow Holy Spirit's command, the atmosphere begins to shift as I unzip my robe. I see from the side that my armor bearer is coming to assist me, but I graciously wave her away.

Pastor has this look of wonderment on his face since Holy Spirit has not shared with him what I am doing.

Underneath my immaculate robe, I am wearing a basic black shirt and skirt. Holy Spirit then tells me to minister what realness really looks like. As I shift the message, the music shifts, the crowd shifts, and now we are in a place of worship.

As Holy Spirit ministers to the congregation, I hear myself tell the crowd to "Keep it Real. To be set free, we must be honest with ourselves." As I continue to minister, what was once praises now have shifted to tears. The altar became crowded with people expressing their admiration for God in hopes of being delivered from whatever bondage that had been holding them captive.

I remember telling them, "The robe is nice, standing here is nice, but if I cannot keep it real with God, my life is not nice." At that moment, I finally understood what God meant by those three powerful words—Keep It Real. I continued by saying, "I first have to be real with myself as I present an imperfect person to an imperfect generation about a perfect God that is able to perfect those things concerning Him." As

I ended the message, prayed for God's people, and watched the power of God transform lives, I realized that God was doing a work in me.

As I took my seat, I thanked God for the manifestation of His Spirit. I realized that the message was not only intended for the congregation but for me to reflect on my life. I thought about how I hid behind so many things, situations, and circumstances that I was not real with God about. I repented to Him for not trusting Him as I should and determined in my mind to give Him all of my cares. As I felt my armor bearer's hands on my back as she prayed, I could hear the continual echoed sound of worship. This is what God wants; the sound of His children crying out to Him. It allowed the Glory of God to rest, move, and saturate us as long as He desired. When I got up off the floor, I sat quietly in the presence of the Lord. Pastor stood at the podium, acknowledging God in all of His splendor. He dismissed the service, turned, and looked at me, and nodded his head in approval. I responded by saying, "To God be all the Glory."

My armor bearer escorted me to my office to assist me in changing my clothes. Few words were exchanged as we were still captivated by the move and awesomeness of God. I handed her a gift in gratitude for her service towards me and hugged her as we exited my office. Mother obtained my attention and called me to her. She poured words of wisdom into my life and explained how much she appreciated me for obeying the voice of God. I gave God all the glory and asked her to continue to pray for me. She stated, "Baby, I never stopped."

My husband met me halfway down the aisle with his arms spread open. I felt my eyes watering because it does something to me when I know he is proud of me. He embraced me, prayed in my ear, and exclaimed his gratitude for being my husband. And again, I cried. I felt my children wrap their arms around my waist. I could remain in that place forever, that place called love.

On our way home, I rehearsed in my mind the word that God brought forth today. It is easy to throw in the towel when you have nothing to lose. God has given us too much to fight for to allow the enemy to take residence in a place where he does not belong. God did not give us the spirit of fear, nor did He give us the spirit to quit. If we maintain the real reason for this journey—souls—we understand that quitting is not an option. I decided to continue the race in which Christ has designed for me and always remember the race is not given to the swift nor the battle to the strong and to endure until the end. I continue to thank God for the words of encouragement as He continues to make, mold, and strengthen the life of this church girl.

ABOUT THE AUTHOR

Latonya P. Grimes was born and raised in Williamston, N.C. She is the mother of three children Joshua, Indiya, and Asiya, who she adores greatly. She is very passionate about her relationship with God and others. Her desire is to ensure that the Kingdom of God prospers and God's children are made free and whole. What brings her joy is watching individuals' transformation as they experience the love and joy of accepting Jesus Christ as their Savior and participating in the work of ministry.

Brought up in the church, Latonya felt the call of ministry at the age of 25. Now under the leadership of Chief Apostle Lannice and Apostle Heather Collins of Kingdom Life Worship Center in Farmville, N.C., she serves as the Overseer/Executive Administrator of Kingdom Covenant International Fellowship of Churches, Inc. and Kingdom Life Worship Center. Working faithfully and tirelessly for God, Latonya birthed her first Women's Conference, entitled: "I Survived," in November 2018. She also is the co-host of the international radio show Lavon Bridgers' Radio Show in Atlanta, Georgia.

Made in the USA
Columbia, SC
08 March 2021

33764990R00055